DEFINITIVE GUIDE FOR GLOBAL HORIZONS

JOSE-NICANOR PINILLA
BARCELONA

DEDICATION

Special dedication to my wife Ana Miriam and my sons Joel and Noah. For more information: www.escueladelemprendedor.com

CONTENTS

ACKNOWLEDGEMENTS

To all the teachers I have had since 1989, when international trade in Spain was not taken into account in the universities. Especially to the precursors of these subjects in Aragon, the International Business School (CESTE) and the University of Wales. I am grateful to all the students I have had for more than 20 years, who have taught me how to teach this subject. Thanks to the support of the School of the Entrepreneur, many teachers and professionals will be able to publish our knowledge in different business management subjects.

1.PROCESS IN GLOBALISATION

Globalisation is a theory whose aims include the interpretation of current events in the fields of development, the world economy, social scenarios, and cultural and political influences. Globalisation is a set of theoretical propositions that emphasise two major trends in particular:

- Global communication systems.
- Economic conditions, especially those related to the mobility of financial and commercial resources.

> Through the process of globalisation, one of the essential assumptions is that more and more nations are relying on integrated conditions of communication, the international financial system and trade. This tends to generate a scenario of greater intercommunication between the world's centres of power and their commercial transactions.

Effects and influences arising from the "integrating aspects" can be studied from two main perspectives:

☐ The external level of countries or systemic level.

☐ The level of internal country conditions or sub-systemic approach. In this case, the units of analysis would be those that correspond to the variables of economic growth and development, as well as social indicators. With regard to the globalisation processes that are currently taking place in the economic sphere, there are two core aspects related to the international economic policy area:

☐ The structure of the global economic system.

☐ And how this structure has changed.

These issues can be addressed on the basis of globalisation theory, taking into account the concepts of development.

> The fundamentals of globalisation point to the world structure and its interrelationships as key elements in understanding the changes occurring at the level of social, political, division of production and particular national and regional conditions.

The fundamental premise of globalisation is that there is a greater degree of integration within and between societies, which plays a major role in the economic and social changes that are taking place. This rationale is widely accepted. However, what is less agreed upon is the mechanisms and principles that govern these changes. Neoclassical economic theories stress the pre-eminence of comparative advantage, international relations methods emphasise geopolitical variables, while perspectives from world systems theory stress unequal exchanges. These approaches offer contrasting interpretations of global change.

More particularly, the main areas of contention in terms of globalisation theory relate to:

- The fact that countries can have more than three areas of placement in the world system: centre, semi-periphery and periphery.
- The characteristics of the position of several countries in terms of sharing the same pattern of relations may be related to the formation of "cliques" or groups with strong or close relations among themselves and weak groupings with the rest, especially at the regional level.
- Even within the same position of countries, e.g. within the periphery, significant variations can be detected between nations, such as size of economies, effective domestic demand, export structure, and levels of economic development.
- There is strong evidence of patterns of economic concentration among nations, especially in the fields of international trade and global finance. Broadly speaking, globalisation has two main meanings:

- ➤ As a phenomenon, it implies that there is an increasing degree of interdependence between different regions and countries of the world, particularly in the areas of trade, financial and communication relations.

> As a theory of development, one of its essential postulates is that a greater level of integration is taking place between different regions of the world, and that this level of integration is affecting the social and economic conditions of countries.

The levels of greater integration mentioned by globalisation are most evident in trade relations, financial flows, tourism and communications. In this sense, the theoretical approach to globalisation draws on elements addressed by world systems theories. However, one of the particular characteristics of globalisation is its emphasis on the elements of communication and cultural aspects.

In addition to technological, financial and political relations, scholars of globalisation argue that important and unprecedented elements of economic communication are taking place between nations. This is evidenced primarily through novel technological processes that enable the interaction of institutions, governments, entities and people around the world.

The main aspects of globalisation are summarised in the following points:

- Global communications systems are becoming increasingly important today; it is through these processes that nations, social groups and individuals are interacting more fluidly both within and between nations.
- Although the most advanced communication systems are operating preferentially among the more developed nations, these mechanisms are also making their effects felt in the less advanced nations. This situation may allow groups from poorer nations to interact with other more developed centres more easily. In this, the touted principle of the global village in terms of communications, trade and financial transactions would make sense to some extent.
- With regard to economic activities, new technological advances in communications are becoming increasingly accessible to local small and medium-sized enterprises. This situation is creating a new scenario for economic transactions, the use of productive resources, equipment, product exchange and the presence of "virtual money mechanisms". . From a cultural perspective, new communication products are developing a pattern of global exchange and interconnection.

- The concept of minorities within different countries is being affected by communication patterns. Although minorities may not be fully integrated into the new communication circuits, they are influenced by the fact that the economically and politically powerful sectors are being integrated into the new sphere of interconnectedness.
- Ultimately the factor that business and political elites determine policy decisions within nation-states continues.
- Economic and social elements that are influenced by the current conditions of the globalisation phenomenon provide circumstances within which social conditions develop within countries.
- Based on the main aspects included in the theory of globalisation, the main assumptions of this theory are summarised as follows:
- Economic and cultural factors are affecting every aspect of social life in an increasingly integrated way.
- Under current conditions and with regard to specific studies of particular spheres of action, such as trade, finance or communications, the unit of analysis based strictly on the concept of the nation-state tends to lose its relevance. In particular, communications are making this category no longer as causally dominant in many aspects of behaviour at the level of nations as it used to be.

In recent years, the term globalisation has been used primarily in connection with the technological revolution in the area of communications and the creation of cyberspace.

It is the functionalist aspect of globalisation that distinguishes the theory from the concept of economic internationalisation. Globalisation contains processes that are qualitatively different from internationalisation. They involve not only the geographical extension of economic activities, processes of internationalisation, but also, and more importantly, the functional integration of previously dispersed activities. The latter being the peculiar feature of globalisation within the most recent technological innovations. The current globalisation process therefore results in the formation of functional units on a planetary level.

> A key feature of globalisation is its emphasis on the study of the increasing integration that emerges between more developed countries. This affects in particular the areas of trade, finance, technology, communications and macroeconomic coordination. In the societies of these countries, there is a phenomenon of social integration, but at the same time increasing discrimination and economic marginalisation among various sectors.

From a more comparative perspective, globalisation theory coincides in certain respects with modernisation theory. One of these aspects is that both approaches establish that the "guiding direction" of development is the conditions of Western Europe and the United States. Emphasis is placed on the fact that the technological advances and accumulation patterns that are established in these development poles are the instruments for achieving better living standards. However, the modernisation perspective differs from globalisation in several respects, including that modernisation follows a more normative exposition, development should follow the "path" of the more developed countries. It indicates what development should look like. Globalisation on the other hand contains a more descriptive and interpretative character based on a more "positive" approach to the phenomena that become evident.

Insofar as globalisation emphasises that economic and cultural aspects determine social processes, this theory offers similar features to those of Max Weber's "comprehensive sociology". In this view, value systems, belief systems and identity patterns are key aspects of understanding social dynamics. Whether these characteristics refer to dominant groups or to subaltern groups within the social context. For globalisation, Weber's approaches of the 1920s need to be adapted to the current conditions of the early 21st century, taking into account the diffusion of ideas, cultural values and the general influence of the media on societies.

The above considerations provide a basis for the assertion that globalisation theory and world systems theory take the global as their fundamental unit of analysis, rather than the category of the nation-state, which is more commonly used in modernisation and dependency studies. The contrasting sense between globalisation and world systems theory, however, is that the latter contains adaptations of dialectical and historical materialist principles, while globalisation emphasises its rather structural and functionalist foundations. Hence, globalists see forms of transformation more in terms of gradual sequences of events than in terms of revolutionary leaps of intense and rapid transformation.

> For globalisation, the challenge for societies is to adapt sequentially to the innovations posed by the new scenarios with their changes in the spheres of communication and the economy.

Globalisation theory, world systems theory and to some extent dependency theory take into account the changes that have occurred most markedly in the economic sphere. For example:

- In March 1973, the governments of the most developed nations began to operate flexible exchange rates in their money markets, which limited the permanence of fixed rate policies for the value of currencies; this condition had a drastic impact on the movement of investments, speculative capital and the placement of resources in bonds and on stock exchanges.

- Since 1976, commercial transactions have reinforced their speculative nature in forward-looking securities, which has been further enhanced by the implementation of technological innovations in the field of information technology and communications.

- The personal computer revolution in the 1980s contributed to a more fluid movement of capital, a situation that was also supported by the fax machine in this decade.

- During the 1990s the main feature has been the promotion of and access to Internet services which has given a character of greater speed and flexibility to intercommunications. It is the Internet that has largely set the scene for a "virtual economy" in recent years, significantly affecting the operations of specific markets.

The main aspects currently under study within the theoretical current of globalisation are:

- New concepts, definitions and empirical evidence related to cultural variables and how they affect national and regional changes.

- Specific processes in which the mechanisms of a "comprehensive sociology" are concentrated within the conditions of the global village.

- Integration at different levels of power both within and between nations and in comparative terms with the different modalities of integration/marginalisation occurring globally.

- Dynamic ways in which new patterns of communication are affecting minority groups within societies.

- Concepts related to the relative autonomy of states and the relationship of states to civil societies, and within that concept, the effectiveness of national decision-making in the macroeconomic field

- Ways in which regionalism and multilateralism are affecting economic and social integration processes.

The process of globalisation represents the most remarkable phase of the world economy in recent years. It consists of a growing union between the basic actors involved in the economic life of a large number of countries. These actors are:

<ul>
<li>✓ Governments. Through liberalisation and integration policies, they make economies more interdependent.</li>
<li>✓ Companies. They seek to improve their processes by relocating part of their resources to countries other than their own.</li>
<li>✓ Consumers. They have very similar tastes due to the media and advertising carried out by multinationals.</li>
</ul>

In the state of the global economy it is necessary to take into account the progress that world production has undergone with the flows of foreign trade and foreign investments. It was from 1960 onwards that foreign trade in goods and services and foreign investment increased rapidly compared to world output. At the beginning of the 21st century, however, international economic relations were far from favourable. It was in 2004 that these foreign relations began to grow again.

The causes of the decline in international economic relations are to be found in a chain of events that have had a negative impact on the world economy, such as political, economic and natural factors.

Political factor: Attack on the Twin Towers in September 2001.

Economic factor: Increase in the price of oil.

Natural factor: Tsunami in Southeast Asia in 2004.

The globalisation of the economy is determined by a series of factors that we will see below:

Political momentum. In recent years, political movements have been very favourable for international relations between countries. More and more nations are opening their doors to the outside world, taking more mature democracies such as those in Europe as a reference point. Recently, in 2011, countries such as Egypt and Tunisia are witnessing massive social movements demanding democracy in their countries. This means that, in the near future, trade relations will be even more fruitful. With the creation of the WTO (World Trade Organisation), formerly GATT (General Agreement on Tariffs and Trade), trade between open and protectionist countries has been boosted exponentially.

Economic integration has favoured the grouping of countries into regional economic blocs. The aim is to open up new markets, make companies more competitive and increase bargaining power vis-à-vis other blocs. An example of this is MERCOSUR. With the fall of the Berlin Wall, many Eastern European countries opened up, establishing a convergence of economic systems. Many of these countries ended up joining the European Union, such as Latvia, Lithuania, Estonia, etc., which has led to the current number of 27 member states.

Improved transport and communications. Today we can safely say that logistics is one of the most important elements of success in international trade. Thanks to the construction of larger and larger ships, we can handle larger volumes, which means that we pass on a very low cost per unit shipped. More than 90% of international trade is carried by sea, although air, rail and road transport are of great importance, as most transport is multimodal. Distances are getting shorter, infrastructures are improving and logistics companies are providing more services for the company, so we no longer have an excuse for not trading with other countries.

Another area worth highlighting is technological and telecommunications advances. The use of the Internet allows instant interaction in terms of any type of communication, whether sending documents or videoconferencing. We should also not forget that nowadays we can even sell our products anywhere in the world through a virtual platform.

Technological change **and company concentration**. Globalisation has unleashed a great deal of competition among companies. It is practically impossible for a micro-company to compete in this market, which is why a minimum size is required for the effective development of certain businesses in certain sectors. Many multinationals are currently in the process of grouping together with other multinationals with the aim of becoming larger and larger. These companies tend to group together in Joint Ventures. This is the recent case of Telefónica's UK subsidiary, O2, Vodafone UK and Everything Everywhere (the partnership formed between Orange and T-Mobile) have joined forces to create a common platform for mobile commerce in the UK.

The global financial market. Today, if there is a globalised sector, it is the financial sector. All analysts agree that this has been the cause of the crisis that we are still suffering in 2011. Capital markets are active 24 hours a day, whether it is London, New York, Frankfurt or Madrid. Interest rates and exchange rates are fully linked, whether it is the EURIBOR market (Euro market) or LIBOR (London convertible currency market). Despite the entry into force of the European Monetary Union in January 1999, no harmonisation of exchange rates has been achieved. The largest volume of international transactions is in euros and dollars, followed by the yen. Despite the small number of currencies, it is not conducive to controlling the exchange rate of these currencies; on the contrary, exchange rate speculation continues on a daily basis.

Multiculturalism. Global commercial exchange favours the homogenisation of culture. Some cultures are predominant, as in the case of the United States, whose capitalist culture has infected the rest of the world. In our capitalist system, based on consumption, it is necessary to have migration flows in developing countries and also a constant flow of immigrants in developed countries to sustain the labour and pension system. In many cities around the world we are getting used to living with citizens of different cultures and ethnicities, although they do not always lose their own cultural traits, as they often settle in ghettos. In terms of languages, the most widely used and internationally recognised language is still English, although Spanish is becoming the second most spoken language in the world. In terms of population, Mandarin Chinese is the most widely spoken language in the world.

Business strategy. Today's companies have the best strategists to compete in international trade. In fact, strategic management is one of the most in-demand positions in large companies. These professionals have to face challenges such as: When will we have to relocate our factory? Which country will we choose? Where will we position ourselves in the target market? It is therefore a question of selecting the most suitable markets and making the most appropriate commercial decisions for the present and the future of the company.

> **Joint Venture**: A type of long-term joint investment business arrangement between two or more companies. In developing countries, it is a collaboration between two companies, with one providing cheap labour and the other providing technology.

2. OFFSHORING AND OUTSOURCING

Within the concept of offshoring we find the following situations:

- ✓ The international displacement of productive activities or relocation from one country to another.
- ✓ It consists of the deindustrialisation resulting from the opening up to international competition.
- ✓ It is an export of jobs, domestic employment is replaced by foreign employment. It does not destroy jobs, but creates them.

> It is not a new phenomenon, but has existed under various forms and names for decades, although not with the dimensions it has acquired today.

During the 1960s and 1970s, the international expansion of large firms was based, above all, on the replication of the same activities in different countries in order to benefit from the expansion of emerging markets and their lower wage costs, circumventing the barriers that protected them from foreign trade competition. Offshoring was not a characteristic phenomenon of this period, nor of the 1980s, when international investment in developing countries slowed down considerably, due to the slow economic growth of the poorest countries, the failure of some of the main strategies aimed at boosting their development and the instability of their institutional and political framework. However, in the 1990s, years of greater economic expansion in developed countries, the drive towards international economic integration (globalisation) and progress in political freedoms and institution-building in many developing countries, the process of offshoring business activities gained momentum.

The reduction of trade barriers, especially tariffs, facilitated entry into various national markets. The increased competitive pressure created by a more global market led to lower costs for firms, including labour costs, and increased the attractiveness of manufacturing in lower-wage areas. In addition, the emergence of large new markets with clear prospects for expansion (China, India and Central and Eastern European countries) offered major business opportunities.

> Offshoring then takes on a predominantly North-South direction, i.e. it involves shifts of production and employment from rich to poor countries.

However, the late 1980s and early 1990s also saw movements in a north-to-north direction, from rich countries to rich countries. In particular, the integration of European economies and the creation of a single market within the European Union favoured this type of relocation. On a global scale, the effects of offshoring are positive in the short and long term. In a process of globalisation, companies relocate where they reduce costs or improve the quality of their products, so that consumers benefit from better and cheaper products. Increased competition favours technological innovation and thus growth in production.

The rapid development of high-population countries such as China and India has counteracted the negative effect on global income distribution of the widening gap between rich and poor. However, offshoring sometimes negatively affects smaller economies. It often occurs in areas where social and political stability is not guaranteed or where remoteness from major markets imposes excessive transport costs, which are not compensated by low wages, as is the case in Africa. The people of these countries are the main victims of globalisation. But a country with a large market can attract foreign companies and encourage them to stay by means of trade tariffs, as in the case of China.

For richer countries, the short-term effects are negative because there are losses of capital and employment, especially of the less skilled. In the long run, however, the effects tend to be beneficial because specialisation in higher quality products is encouraged and more ambitious training plans are put in place. These economies also benefit in the long run from the expansion of global demand and production. However, the negative short-term effects also depend on the way in which offshoring takes place. It is not the same whether it is carried out by domestic or foreign companies. The former establish productive links of complementarity with their subsidiaries in the rest of the world, and it does not seem as clear-cut as it is believed that they replace internal jobs with external ones.

This phenomenon has so far affected the manufacturing sectors, but is tending to spread to the services sector, supported by information and communication technologies, which allow the relocation of administrative processes to lower-wage countries.

> Examples of this are the so-called call centres of telephone companies, or the applications and computer processing departments of these same companies, airlines or banks. This modern type of offshoring is all the more worrying and surprising because until now it was thought that services were relatively shielded from international competition.

Advances in new technologies make it possible to isolate business areas that are not directly related to the supply of the service (administrative tasks) or that can be carried out remotely by telematic means, and to outsource them to other companies in the country or elsewhere, or simply to offshore them. Despite the alarm caused by this process, there are no precise data on its quantitative importance, beyond the suspicion that it has grown very strongly, in parallel with foreign direct investment (FDI).

However, it is not known how much of the investment directed to developing countries can be qualified as offshoring, and the extent to which this phenomenon accompanies the international restructuring of large firms' production through mergers and takeovers.

A more accurate approximation is obtained through the individual cases of countries and companies. In Spain, information is available from the Foreign Investment Register of the Ministry of Economy, which makes it possible to estimate disinvestment in foreign capital. However, disinvestment does not always reflect a process of relocation. Sometimes foreign investors simply reduce their stake in a company's capital, which is then taken over by Spaniards. Others backtrack on their initial plans, before starting production activities, when they have a better knowledge of the domestic market. Or they restructure their companies' products, abandoning certain lines, not only in the country but also on a global scale. Or they simply fail in the face of domestic competition and have to close established subsidiaries.

In any case, the growing disinvestment of foreign capital in Spain since 1993 is a fact. It is also a fact that, until now, it has been globally compensated by the flow of new direct investment, albeit to an increasingly lesser extent. Moreover, not in all sectors is such compensation taking place, so that foreign money seems to be decreasing its presence in some technology-intensive fields of industry such as computers and precision instruments.

There is no hard data because there is no information on investments made in Spain by foreign-owned companies with funds that do not come from abroad (local loans or reinvested profits). Moreover, offshoring does not only refer to these companies. Domestic companies also relocate, although to a lesser extent and in different ways, which corroborates the limited evidence available for other countries.

Offshoring has not prevented sustained growth in advanced economies so far, nor will it do so in the future. But it will lead to increased specialisation in high technology.

> Between 1990 and 1995, there were 174 cases of relocation, 100 of which were in Spain. Of the total, only 19 involved the closure of the facilities; 19 others were taken over by national owners. In the others, product lines or specific facilities were closed. Of the cases in Spain, 75% were foreign firms and the rest belonged to Spaniards and were located in the more traditional sectors (food, footwear, textiles).

Behind the figures lies a significant reduction in foreign ownership and a considerable number of company closures. However, the dominant trend was the closure of product lines and production establishments in the larger companies, which concentrated their activities on fewer products and fewer establishments. Relocation should be understood within a framework of growing international competition that drives companies to acquire new competitive advantages (cost or otherwise) and to be present in rapidly expanding markets. sión. This does not mean, as some suggest, that such virtues are found only in the less developed countries, and therefore that the process of offshoring radically threatens the productive fabric and employment in the more advanced countries.

It is true that low wages have a great attraction. But labour is not the only factor that defines the cost function of firms, nor is it the most important in the production of superior quality products, where innovation and skilled labour also play a central role. The spatial environment in which production takes place is also crucial for its efficiency and competitiveness. The legal security of a regulatory framework; the competitive incentive and technological advantages offered by a vibrant business fabric; economies of scale, which allow proximity to a large market, and cost reduction, which are facilitated by adequate transport infrastructures, are decisive aspects.

Most of these favourable environmental conditions are agglomeration economies, i.e. advantages derived from concentrating many productive establishments in a small space, from forming large industrial masses in a given area. They are the result of economic development. In terms of advantages, we can cite the high qualification of the workforce and a high technological effort. These industrial groupings are called "*clusters*".

> To define "cluster" there is nothing like an example: Silicon Valley or Hollywood. It is a geographical concentration of interconnected companies, specialised suppliers, service providers, etc. that compete, but also cooperate. It is the interaction of skills and the sum of efforts of many companies. They arise because they encourage competition and interaction. They also encourage links and informal dealings between enterprises and institutions. All this fosters innovation.

For medium-high developing economies, such as Spain's, the threats come not only from the more backward countries, but also from the more advanced ones with better-trained workers and greater economies of agglomeration. The greatest danger comes from the new EU partners, thanks to their special combination of low wages and highly skilled labour.

In the 1990s offshoring was basically due to low wage costs in traditional manufacturing sectors (textiles, clothing, footwear, toys), the main destinations being Portugal, Morocco, Romania, China and some Latin American countries.

On the other hand, offshored companies in the most technologically advanced sectors, all of them foreign-owned, moved to other developed countries, almost always from the EU, often approaching the Old Continent's centre rich in agglomeration economies.

There seems to be a clear divide between Spanish disinvestment and investment in other central and eastern European countries. Companies producing automobiles and components, steel products and other basic metals do not seem to be seduced by Eastern European countries, although the threat always remains latent (the electronic components company ACE moved its production to Mexico and Romania).

What may apparently be a threat to Spain is foreign disinvestment in companies in technology sectors, where the international investments received have not been able to compensate for the disinvestments, resulting in a net loss. Some of the best known cases are those of Alcatel, Ericsson, Delphi and Valeo. On other occasions, production activities have been closed down because ownership has passed into the hands of Spanish shareholders. For example, Pfizer was taken over by Farmasierra and Glaxo by Alcalá Farma, both Spanish companies being subcontractors of these multinationals. In other sectors, the disinvestment of foreign capital responds to the good performance and efficiency of Spanish companies, often buyers of foreign shareholdings (Argal and Fontaneda by Spanish food groups). In short, only by investing in technological research and skilled labour will Spain maintain a promising future.

The countries that have received the most offshored companies in recent years have been Ireland, Canada, Israel and India. These accounted for 70% of the world market for offshored services. Call centres are concentrated in developed world countries. However, there is a general tendency to invest in developing countries in order to gain a strategic position for the future, to shift activity to new products and to conquer new markets.

The main offshored activities are those related to Information Technology: Call Centres, Shared Services Centres and Information Technology Services (software development, consultancy...).

It can be observed that the dominant countries in receiving offshoring are countries with English as the main language of business. In general, English is a prevailing factor when it comes to choosing the "locality" in which to provide services. This ensures an improvement in the quality of the services provided by having better communication.

The most important host country is currently India (and South East Asia) for several factors: language, low labour costs, high graduation and qualification of employees and high IT expertise. Other important countries are Canada, Ireland and Australia, which, although they do not have such low wage costs, offer unbeatable infrastructure and technical capabilities.

On the other hand, the countries of Eastern Central Europe are benefiting greatly from this offshoring trend. The entry of these countries into the EU is a fact to be taken into account in the near future since, being within the Union, the procedures and legal requirements are streamlined, making it much easier to outsource certain services from the Union itself. Hungary and the Czech Republic are currently the most attractive countries due to their language skills, lower information privacy barriers, stable socio-political environment and higher technical capabilities.

In Latin America, Brazil, Mexico and Chile are the main beneficiaries of offshoring, mainly due to low costs and social and economic stability.

> 83% of companies in Europe that have offshored are satisfied with this activity, and 44% plan to continue offshoring in the future. In other words, offshoring figures are expected to continue to rise.

Offshoring offers brakes and advantages to both service-exporting and service-receiving countries:

- ➤ The brakes on offshoring are:
- ➤ Market distancing.
- ➤ Lack of personal contact with customers.
- ➤ Trust in suppliers (due to culture, tradition...).
- ➤ Lack of international recognition of staff qualifications.
- ➤ Technological gap in the country importing the services.
- ➤ Legislation and regulation of business activities differ from country to country.

- ➢ Increased costs and transaction times depending on the services.
- ➢ Social restraint on the part of the country of origin that leads to alarms when there are mass redundancies or job uncertainty, causing "drastic measures" to be taken in human resources policies in order to save jobs, as well as a bad image and mistrust of the company and the system in general. This also causes mobility to other places to find work and the need for retraining and re-training of staff. Therefore, the transition process is not as straightforward as it may seem at first.
- ➢ The advantages of offshoring are:
    - ✓ For the country of origin:
    - ✓ Cost reduction, especially due to low labour costs. This is actually the main reason for companies to relocate.
    - ✓ Offshoring companies can divert attention and efforts away from more mechanical tasks and focus on more skill-intensive and value-adding actions, such as research and development.
    - ✓ Improving the quality of the services provided by being more specialised.
    - ✓ Improvement of the company's competitiveness, with the following positive effects in its country of origin.
    - ✓ Workers become more skilled and specialised.
    - ✓ Improving the competitiveness of Human Resources.
    - ✓ Improving Information Technology for better communication.
    - ✓ For the host country:
    - ✓ Increase in export earnings.
    - ✓ Job creation.
    - ✓ Higher wages.
    - ✓ Workers become more skilled and specialised.
- ➢ Improving the competitiveness of Human Resources.
- ➢ Improving Information Technology for better communication.

3. INTERNATIONAL EXCHANGES

Trade should be seen as the economic nexus between production, consumption and investment. The consumer is supplied with goods and becomes the last stage of the production process. Foreign trade can be considered as a technique of foreign trade. It encompasses the set of exchange relations of goods and commercial services of a country with foreign partners, through sales or purchases that originate credits of obligations in foreign currency and euros, a relationship that implies national and international legal obligations. A national economy that goes beyond the borders of the state can be described as a foreign trade circulation. Through this extraterritorial process, the national division of labour expands and leads to the global economy.

> Today's foreign trade is based on a system of free trade that is totally opposed to a protectionist system (protection of national production and trade), which protects and stimulates the circulation of trade free of restrictive measures or barriers that hinder the free international exchange of goods and services. It is a fact that trade relations have a favourable influence on the economic life of each country.

In the second half of the 20th century, the international division of labour proved to be a useful tool for many national economies to progress. The benefits of international trade helped to consolidate countries' economic structures. This evolution is reflected in world trade production, which has gone from a factor of 8.6 in the 1950s to a factor of 30 in 2007. We can highlight the increase in the world GDP from 28% in 1970 to almost 50% today.

All exported or imported goods are subject to a customs declaration. In Spain, this is instrumented in the DUA (Documento Único Administrativo) (Single Administrative Document). This declaration allows us to know the origin and destination of the goods, the declared value, who is buying and who is selling, etc. Since 1 January 1993, fiscal frontiers have disappeared in the European Union, establishing a common market for trade between member states. Now we are no longer talking about imports and exports, but about intra-Community acquisitions and deliveries. The European Union's leadership in international trade has been demonstrated by its strong currency and its importance in international trade (it accounts for 40% of world trade).

In fact, the European currency has become a powerful international currency, used as a unit of account on the world market against the US dollar or the Japanese yen. The fluctuations it has experienced over the last ten years with respect to the dollar have positioned the euro as a reference currency in international trade, despite speculative attempts to devalue the currency and turbulence caused by the Greek and Portuguese crises, as well as Ireland.

> In a study by the International Monetary Fund in April 2010, the experts point to the replacement of the dollar by a universal currency called *bancor*. Its main function would be to establish itself as a global exchange currency issued by the World Bank.

In the following table we can analyse what the exchange of goods and services entails, the main developed areas in the world being the United States, the European Union and Japan: United States, European Union and Japan.

These are: United States, Germany, Japan, France, United Kingdom, Canada, Italy and China, covering between them almost 55% of the global value of goods and services.

Analysing the evolution of Spanish foreign trade over the last decade, it is relatively positive in terms of progression. Between 1988 and 2004, there was a 4.6-fold increase, which implies a respectable annual progression, although with a permanent trade deficit. Spain has an intense activity within the European Union, with an annual average of approximately 68%. With America and Asia it accounts for 10%.

China and India play a significant role in the dynamism of international trade. India's demographics are evolving rapidly, with 1.2 billion consumers (17% of the world's population). It is also becoming increasingly important economically. China, with a population of more than 1.3 billion (20% of the world's population), ranks third in terms of GDP. Thanks to the policy of economic liberalisation it embarked on more than 30 years ago, China is experiencing annual economic growth of around 10%.

In 2008, in the context of the global crisis, developing countries began to emerge from the crisis, while the more industrialised countries entered a process of economic decline. In 2010, some countries such as China, India and Indonesia grew by more than 5 per cent. Others such as Egypt and Brazil remain unchanged. In high-income countries, however, the crisis has really hit home. GDP growth averages 4% in countries such as the US, Germany, France, Italy, Spain, Japan, etc.

This impact has been detrimental to international trade, which is experiencing a decline of more than 14%, making it the Achilles heel of the most industrialised economies. From 2011 onwards, new forms of international trade will appear, thanks to new technologies and a change of awareness in most societies on this planet, which will have repercussions on a new economic and social configuration on a global level.

4. DIFFERENCES IN MARKETS

We have talked extensively about the concept of globalisation, especially as it affects the economy. But there are also opportunities that favour the localisation of business activity, so that companies operating in small geographical areas can compete with multinationals. Normally we can think of large transnational companies as monopolising all foreign markets, offering the same product in a multitude of local markets. This is possible because of the large investments they make in the expansion of their products in each continent, contributing a large part of their budget to their communication policy. We have also mentioned the homogenisation of consumer tastes. Purchasing decisions are strongly influenced by the personal characteristics of buyers. When this behaviour occurs repeatedly in a large population group, we speak of consumer habits. Even in apparently homogeneous countries.

> Washbasins in the UK have two taps, however, in Western Europe the single lever has become the norm.

However, throughout international trade we will find opportunities, in different markets and different consumers. The cultural environments in each country are very different, therefore, in order to introduce our products in these markets, we must avoid the barriers that our ethnocentrism causes us. In the same way, it is advisable to avoid the pernicious clichés and traditional stereotypes that the countries of the world apply to each other.

One of the aspects that most influences the difference between countries is their level of wealth and per capita income. We all know that the world's wealth is in the hands of a few. Eighty per cent of the world's wealth is concentrated in 25 countries, mainly the United States and Canada, Western Europe and Japan.

One of the values to consider when planning entry into a foreign market is the average per capita income of the citizen. We find abysmal differences in the annual income of citizens from African countries (some with incomes of 600 dollars a year) to Arab countries such as Qatar with a per capita income of more than 75,000 dollars a year. There are also differences in income distribution: lower-middle income countries such as China, Brazil, Mexico and Russia have a very small percentage of the population with a very high purchasing power.

> Economic differences can also be found in the growth progression of developing countries. The clearest example is China, which is growing at an average of around 10% per year.

Another relevant aspect is the cultural differences found in countries. Traditions and values educate the beliefs of all citizens. In Western societies, the capitalist creed has prevailed, although we realise that Eastern countries that are beginning their economic expansion admit this creed in the same way. According to Hall, cultural differences are high-context and low-context. High-context cultures are societies that need to express a message reiteratively, which disperses communication. Mediterranean and Latin societies can be placed within this context. However, low-context cultures, such as Nordic countries, Germany, etc. need to express little in order to say a lot.

The Dutch anthropologist and writer Hofstede analysed 70 countries of different cultures and simplified complex socio-cultural patterns of behaviour into five simple indicators:

- Power distance: The degree of inequality among people, what a country's population considers to be the norm.
- Individualism versus collectivism: The degree to which they feel they must care or be cared for themselves, their families or the organisations to which they belong.
- . Masculinity versus femininity: The degree to which a culture is conducive to domination, to the acquisition of things. Versus a culture that is more inclined to people, assertiveness, sensation and quality of life.
- Uncertainty avoidance: The degree to which people in a country prefer structured situations over unstructured situations.
- Long-term versus short-term orientation: Long-term oriented cultures are cultures that look to the future, such as thrift and persistence. Short-term oriented cultures have values that look to the past and present, such as respect for tradition and the fulfilment of social obligations. In societies such as Japan and Germany, savings are valued, while Mediterranean countries are more inclined towards consumption.

> As far as cultural differences are concerned, we can find very curious cases, for example, that in Bulgaria the gestures of negation and affirmation are reversed.

Another difference between cultures is the religious orientation, which is the result of years of tradition in the religious institutions of each country. For example, we can cite the Arab culture, which acts with scrupulous zeal and compliance with the Muslim religion, through the fundamental law of the state, which is Islamic law (Sharia). This means that imports of alcohol, pork, gambling articles (except cards), zoomorphic or anthropomorphic sculptures, pornographic material, etc. are prohibited.

One of the cultures in conflict with Arab countries is Israel, which is steeped in the Jewish religion with a millennia-long tradition. This is reflected in trade with other countries. For example, imports of meat and meat products require *kashrut* and *kosher* certification and must be approved by the Chief Rabbinate with regard to ingredients and manufacturing processes.

The Hebrew word kosher means fit. The laws of kashrut define the foods that are fit for consumption by a Jew.

Among the cultural differences, language is perhaps the most important. The number of recognised languages in the world is around 6,909 languages, so we deduce that there are several languages in different countries, as there are approximately 200 countries in the world. English and Spanish have become the two languages of reference, although Mandarin Chinese is the most widely spoken language in the world. When a company begins the process of internationalisation, it must take into account how it focuses its communication policy, therefore, the chosen language is a fundamental part of the commercial strategy of any company. All commercial documentation (pro forma invoices, contracts, etc.), transport documentation, customs documentation, etc. must be adapted. You must also do this with promotional documentation, catalogues and, above all, perfectly delimit the markets you are targeting through the chosen languages. This is evident in any online platform project, as it is essential to offer quality information in local languages.

One of the barriers faced by small businesses in Spain is the lack of professionalism when it comes to speaking a foreign language. The level of managers is improving all the time, especially with European languages such as English, French or German, although we are taking steps to learn other very competitive languages such as Mandarin Chinese.

The legal framework for foreign trade and foreign investment operations would be another aspect to consider. Thanks to bilateral agreements between countries and framework agreements established in geographical and continental areas (European Union, MERCOSUR), the harmonisation of laws is gradually being integrated into economic blocs. However, international legislation remains a stumbling block that is sometimes difficult to overcome. In many cases, the different legislations create technical barriers to the entry of products for foreign companies.

> Basically, three types of barriers can be distinguished:
>
> **Fiscal**: Import duties and taxes.
>
> **Quantitative**: Quotas that set limits on the maximum quantities to be imported.
>
> **Technicians**: Sanitation, Quality Control, Health or Environment certifications.

5. RIVALRY BETWEEN LARGE AND SMALL COMPANIES

Many of the companies that currently have a higher degree of internationalisation began their exports with stock that they could not sell on the domestic market. This was a way of reducing stocks that could only be sold in less developed, i.e. less demanding, markets. These companies turned to foreign markets as a consequence of adverse conditions in the domestic market. In a recessionary economic situation, such as the current one, companies consider the foreign alternative as a temporary means of survival.

> In the case of Spain, companies have historically developed in a limited and protected market. The lack of real competition allowed situations of low productivity, both in terms of labour and capital, lack of business culture and management techniques. On the other hand, well-managed companies with a business culture and brand image, as well as a significant share of the national market, were acquired by multinationals whose objective was to establish themselves in our market.

With full integration into the European Union, Spanish companies had to compete in a foreign market. Some disappeared due to lack of adaptation and others developed the procedures of a company in the process of internationalisation. Those were times when going abroad was not part of the company's expansion plan, but rather sporadic contacts with foreign clients. Nowadays, the internationalisation process of the company must be an indispensable component for the evolution of the business. This need to go abroad is due to the advantages from a production, commercial, financial or human resources point of view.

Obtaining competitive advantages in production is a good incentive to go to other markets. Many sectors have moved their production to developing countries, with much lower wages, which allows them to obtain a competitive advantage through costs. This is very common in sectors with low value-added products such as textiles.

Large multinationals operate in sectors that need abundant natural resources and raw materials. For example, the oil and coffee sectors, which invest heavily in countries where these raw materials are found in large quantities. The company, when it already has international experience, tries to make the most of the competitive advantages of each country in the different phases of activity. These are companies that manufacture products that are previously designed, produced and assembled in different countries, depending on the advantages offered in each of the aforementioned processes.

Commercially, the export process means accessing a wider market made up of specific segments in each product. If we manage to be present in a large number of countries, the life cycle of our product can be extended, because when the product is in a phase of maturity or decline in developed markets, we can access other markets where the product still has the potential to be re-launched. In these new markets the company will not have to face as many competitors as in the domestic market, and therefore has the possibility to increase its sales turnover.

The emergence of economic blocs such as the European Union has led to increased competition mainly due to excess production capacity, and therefore the need to sell at any price. Most markets are saturated. Product life cycles are becoming shorter and shorter. Buyers are more demanding. Against this backdrop, the future does not look bright for small companies, as they do not invest as much in innovation and development. However, it has facilitated the incorporation of SMEs that are learning to operate in these markets, traditionally the scene of multinationals.

> With more than 20 million enterprises in the private sector in the European Union, excluding the primary sector, more than 98% are SMEs, especially in Italy and Spain.

The need to be in contact with the customer is one of the good reasons to internationalise, as the delivery of the product or service requires added value in the provision of services to the customer, so that they have the feeling that we are close to them, through a branch or representative. After-sales service is essential to build customer loyalty and to stay in the market. The SME must acquire a greater degree of commitment in its international activity, by carrying out an internal analysis in which weaknesses and strengths are identified in order to be able to compete with solvency. The internationalisation process must start from each of the areas of the company and try to grow in the same way. In terms of external factors, the company will be subject to certain cultural conditioning factors of the market where we are trying to sell. There are groups of consumers who tend to buy national products because of their protectionist nature or because they think that the national product is of better quality. This dynamic in the face of the rejection of foreign products can be observed with Asian products in the West, especially with Chinese products. One way to improve the image of the product and eliminate cultural barriers is to move part of the production and distribution to the country of destination, thus overcoming protectionist barriers.

> One of the key reasons for a company to internationalise into several markets is *risk diversification*.

In short, internationalisation offers a wide range of advantages that affect all areas of the company. Knowing at first hand how the company is evolving in the different foreign markets, as well as the continuous adaptation of the company to the tastes of foreign consumers, will turn the company into a more competitive business in the medium term and its strategies can be standardised in order to cover more and more markets and develop an optimal economy of scale.

5.1. THE MULTINATIONAL ENTERPRISE

A multinational company is one that has permanent units, either through branches or commercial subsidiaries or production subsidiaries in more than one country. We could speak of companies that began the process of internationalisation some time ago and have already established themselves in international trade. Historically, multinational companies began to appear at the end of the 19th century. They were benchmark companies in the domestic market and considered broadening their horizons in foreign markets. Above all, the sectors that began to internationalise the fastest were the industrial sectors, including the automotive industry.

One might think that the rationale for multinational companies lies in obtaining economies of scale and taking advantage of a favourable supply of raw materials, energy resources or cheap labour. But the fundamental basis is to expand the number of customers and their turnover. From a strategic and organisational point of view, three dimensions of international companies can be identified:

- The international company: A company that grants limited independence to its subsidiaries. Decisions are highly centralised in the parent company. The development of the company takes place in the country of origin.
- The multinational company: This company grants freedom of movement to its subsidiaries in terms of commercial and expansion strategies. R&D&I activities are usually centralised, although other activities such as production, purchasing and marketing are often decentralised. A good example of this type of company is the automotive industry.
- Transnational company: In this type of company, its subsidiaries are at the same level as the parent company. The policies and strategies developed in these subsidiaries provide the added value that the company needs and become a global competitive advantage. We can cite several examples: ZARA, BANCO SANTANDER, etc.

6.INTERNATIONAL ECONOMIC ORGANISATIONS

In recent years, the creation of multilateral economic organisations and the signing of international agreements have contributed to the development of international trade, especially in aspects such as the reduction of tariffs and quotas, promoting the liberalisation of capital markets. It is therefore advisable for the company to be aware of the functioning of these institutions as part of the expansion strategy. Despite the arguments of free trade, countries tend to implement protectionist measures to defend their markets against international competition, especially in times of economic crisis.

As a consequence of the world wars, protectionist processes developed in many countries, especially in Europe. They soon realised that with free trade the economy could develop much faster. It all began with the Bretton Woods agreements, which resulted in the International Monetary Fund and the World Bank. For the first time an institution appeared that would regulate world trade. One of the problems that could not be tackled was the high cost of tariffs. As a result of a meeting of 23 countries on 30 October 1947, the General Agreement on Tariffs and Trade (GATT) was signed.

> The working principle of GATT refers to the most-favoured-nation clause: it means that contracting parties are obliged to grant each other treatment equally favourable to that which they grant to another member country of the Agreement in their trade relations.

Another principle that was signed was that of transparency. Governments undertook to eliminate all types of non-tariff barriers and replace them with tariff barriers. The principle of non-discrimination aims to eliminate policies that alter trade competition between countries (dumping). One of the last treaties was preferential treatment for developing countries through enabling clauses for multilateral agreements, trade restrictive measures for balance of payments reasons and safeguard measures for development reasons.

6.1. THE GATT AND THE URUGUAY ROUND

The Uruguay Round was the last and most ambitious of the negotiations. A total of 117 countries participated in the negotiations. The negotiations were very intense and were delayed by the EU and the United States over the reduction of barriers and subsidies for agricultural products. With the signing of the Uruguay Round agreements, the WTO (World Trade Organisation) was created on 1 January 1995. This institution will be responsible for ensuring the development and liberalisation of world trade, enforcing the Uruguay Round agreements and administering bodies such as the Council for Trade in Goods, the Council for Trade in Services and the Council for Intellectual Property Rights.

> The main problem facing the WTO is the different perspective of developing countries and countries with stronger economies. The former are trying to export their agricultural products and raw materials to rich countries, while the latter are trying to liberalise markets for capital goods, services and capital.

Over the last ten years, there have been a multitude of negotiations, although the results have been very limited. Since Seattle, Doha (2001), Cancun (2003), Davos (several years), Havana (2010) and many other cities have tried to solve a multitude of economic and trade problems between member countries.

6.2. UNCTAD

Most developing countries were already members of GATT. Since they did not consider it to be the right framework, the United Nations Conference on Trade and Development (UNCTAD) was created in 1964. It works on two main issues:

- Common Fund for Commodities: The aim is to keep commodity prices stable through international commodity agreements, making it possible for producer countries to control supply and demand.

- Generalised System of Preferences: The aim was to enable developing countries to export manufactures to industrialised countries at zero or very low tariffs.

6.3. THE INTERNATIONAL MONETARY FUND

The International Monetary Fund was created together with the World Bank at Bretton Woods in July 1944. It currently has 187 members. Its main purpose is to ensure the stability of the international monetary system (international payments system and exchange rates). One of its main objectives is to promote sustainable economic growth, improve living standards and reduce poverty.

The IMF established a monetary system based on fixed exchange rates, but adjustable depending on circumstances. The parity of the currency was fixed in terms of its gold content. The parity of gold with currencies could not be changed and the authorities of each country were committed to keeping it within a 1% band. This rigidity led to inflation problems and balance of payments imbalances.

> In the case of the dollar, one ounce of fine gold (31.10 grams) was worth $35.

After a speculative attack on the dollar in the early 1970s, it was decided to suspend the convertibility of the dollar into gold and a devaluation of 10% against gold and indirectly against other currencies such as the pound, the yen or the Swiss franc was agreed. In the end it was decided to have a "dirty" float, i.e. controlled by the central banks of all currencies. Over time, this has led to many exchange rate fluctuations and a monetary system that is very closely tied to the dollar, although the euro is now taking on a certain preponderance on the international market. Despite its status as guarantor of international finance, the IMF has not been able to solve three major problems:

- Exchange rate volatility.
- Foreign debt in developing countries, as well as the huge debt that many developed countries (the United States and some EU countries) carry.
- Trade imbalances.

6.4. WORLD BANK AND REGIONAL DEVELOPMENT BANKS

One of the World Bank's main functions is to provide medium and long-term financial resources for investment projects in developing countries. To this end, it uses its own resources and issues placed by the World Bank's Partner States.

> To join the World Bank you need to be a member of the IMF.

The World Bank implements numerous projects and provides a wide range of analytical and advisory services to help countries and the international community respond to their development needs. Support is channelled through the four institutions that make up the World Bank:

- International Bank for Reconstruction and Development (IBRD). For market-based lending to developing countries you comment on per-capita averages.
- International Development Association (IDA). It provides interest-free or below-market concessional loans.
- International Finance Corporation (IFC). Supports private sector initiatives.
- Multilateral Investment Guarantee Agency (MIGA).

It provides guarantees to cover non-commercial risks in private sector investments. There are other multilateral institutions that complement the World Bank, such as the Inter-American Development Bank (IDB), the Asian Development Bank (ADB), the African Development Bank (AfDB) and the European Bank for Reconstruction and Development (EBRD) . The EBRD was created to assist Eastern European countries in their transition process. All these institutions stimulate the level of economic activity in the most disadvantaged countries. Often the only way to attract trade and foreign exchange.

6.5. THE OECD

The Organisation for Economic Co-operation and Development was established on 30 September 1961 by the countries of Western Europe, the United States, Canada, Japan, Australia and New Zealand. The Organisation for European Economic Co-operation, which was established in 1947 to carry out the reconstruction of Europe through the Marshall Plan, was left behind. With the accession of Canada and the United States, the OECD was born. Originally, in 1960, there were 18 European countries plus the United States and Canada. Today it has 34 members, most of them economically advanced countries as well as emerging countries such as Mexico, Chile and Turkey. The giants China, India and Brazil are also members.

> The OECD budget in 2011 is €342 million. The largest contribution is made by the United States with 24%, followed by Japan.

Another of the institutions with great global power is the G7, made up of the finance ministers of the United States, Canada, Japan, Germany, France, Great Britain and Italy, as well as Russia, which meets as the G8 to agree on economic policy issues in times of crisis.

7. ECONOMIC INTEGRATION

In recent years one of the most important developments in the world economy has been the integration of countries into regional economic blocs of which the European Union is the most advanced and successful process so far. Integration changes the environment in which companies carry out their activities and, as a consequence, has an effect on international marketing strategies.

> In a free trade region, distribution will be concentrated in well-located countries with good logistical infrastructure to achieve economies of scale and benefit from the free movement of goods.

Integration also means increased competition, with large industrial groups being obliged to manufacture in one of the countries that are signatories to the Agreement. As the variations between markets disappear, a more uniform marketing mix can be achieved: the unification of legislation will allow the use of a single packaging and labelling, or an exclusive registration of trademarks and patents for all countries. For these reasons, it is essential for companies to be aware of the advantages of the different types of integration, as well as to understand the current situation of integration processes in more advanced stages, mainly in Europe and America.

> ***Integration*** is a process whereby two or more separate national markets that are considered insufficient or inadequate in size enter into agreements to form a single, larger market.

Integration usually takes place through customs tariffs and multilateral trade regimes, protectionist mechanisms for domestic economies. Four possible forms of integration can be distinguished:

- ➢ Preferential customs systems: Countries that grant tariff advantages. The European Union maintains a generalised preferential system with Mediterranean countries, EFTA and ACP countries in particular. China has obtained around 25% of tariff reductions in recent years.
- ➢ Free trade areas: These are areas made up of several countries that maintain their own customs tariffs and trade regime (EFTA: Switzerland, Iceland, Liechtenstein and Norway).
- ➢ Customs unions: This involves the immediate removal of tariff and trade barriers. For example, the European Customs Union.
- ➢ Economic unions: The aim is to eliminate the disparity between social and economic policies. Full economic union is achieved through the unification of monetary, fiscal and income policies and the creation of a single currency. Again, the European Union is an example of this.

7.1. EUROPEAN UNION

It is a process of integration that has achieved great cohesion, even leading to a common market (Economic and Monetary Union). The integration of the European Union has taken place in three phases:

- **Common Market**: The origin of the EU was the creation of the European Community, which itself consisted of three Communities:
- The ECSC (European Coal and Steel Community).
- EURATOM (European Atomic Energy Community).
- The EEC (European Economic Community).

> The basic objective of the European Community was the creation of a customs union between the six countries that signed the founding treaty: Belgium, France, Germany, Italy, Luxembourg and the Netherlands. Subsequently, the United Kingdom, Ireland, Denmark, Greece, Spain, Portugal, Austria, Sweden and Finland joined.

This customs union was known as the Common Market and constituted the elimination of tariffs and quotas on trade between EU countries, as well as the establishment of a Common External Tariff for products from countries outside the European Community.

Single European Market: This is a further step towards the common market or customs union. The member countries established a compromise on four single freedoms:

Free movement of goods. Since 1993, goods have circulated without administrative controls at the border. In the past, all these formalities were carried out at customs, today they are carried out at the offices of exporters and importers, as long as it is between EU countries. VAT is not paid at the border either, but when the quarterly declaration is made. Veterinary, phytosanitary and technical checks on vehicles are now carried out within the member states. All of this has reduced customs congestion and improved the fluidity of intra-Community goods traffic. Another aspect that has been put in common is the unification of technical and manufacturing processes, in terms of the composition of products and standards of approval and certification, thus eliminating technical barriers between EU countries.

Free movement of services. This is a partial liberalisation, as only transport and financial services have been liberalised to a greater extent.

Free movement of capital. Companies and citizens can make unlimited transfers of funds between member states. However, in the case of Spain it is compulsory to report financial transactions with EU countries.

Free movement of persons. EU citizens can travel freely within the EU, without internal border controls. It also means that any EU worker can provide services in any EU country.

> The achievement of this objective has been delayed as the recognition of diplomas and the granting of residence and work permits to EU citizens by other Member States has not yet been completed.

Economic and Monetary Union: At the end of 1993 the Treaty on European Union enters into force with the aim of strengthening the process of European integration. The European Community is renamed the European Union. This new name reflects the basic objective of progress in the integration process: the creation of an Economic and Monetary Union.

As of 1 January 1999 the euro becomes the currency of 11 Member States. The transitional period ends on 1 January 2002. Euro banknotes and coins start to circulate in domestic and international trade. From 30 June 2002 the exchange period ends, national currencies lose their legal tender status. From then on they cannot be used, although they can be exchanged at the central banks of each member state.

7.2. EASTERN EUROPE

In 1949 the Council for Mutual Economic Assistance (COMECON) was created, whose founding countries were the USSR, Poland, Czechoslovakia, Hungary, Romania and Bulgaria. Later, in 1973, Cuba joined. After the dissolution of the USSR, and by default of COMECON, most of its member countries decided to look to the European Union for their future. From 1995 onwards, Czechoslovakia, Poland and Hungary already had zero tariffs on trade flows. This was extended to Bulgaria and Romania.

> Romania and Bulgaria join the European Union on 1 January 2007, making it an entity of 27 Member States and almost 500 million citizens.

7.3. AMERICA

On 1 October 1987 a free trade agreement was signed between the United States and Canada. The elimination of tariffs between the two countries will take place over a period of 10 years with safeguard clauses on exports of products imported from third countries requiring sufficient domestic processing. Investments from the other country are considered as domestic, thus eliminating restrictions on investment by new companies.

NAFTA. In 1989, the agreement between the United States and Canada officially began to be known as the North American Free Trade Agreement (NAFTA), which Mexico joined in June 1991. This treaty includes agreements on market access, trade rules, services, investment, intellectual property and dispute settlement. On the one hand, Mexico shares this agreement with two of the world's most developed countries, and the United States fears its effects on cheap and plentiful employment in Mexico.

> As a result of the treaty, one of the examples of collaboration in the business economy would be the agreement between WALT MART (American department store) and the Mexican discount supermarket chain CIFRA.

Latin America. There are several treaties and partnerships that respond to the palpable differences in the economies of Latin American countries:

ALADI: Latin American Integration Association. Made up of Argentina, Bolivia, Brazil, Colombia, Chile, Mexico, Ecuador, Uruguay, Peru and Venezuela.

MERCOSUR: Common Market of the Southern Cone. Formed in March 1991 by Brazil, Argentina, Paraguay and Uruguay. These four countries account for 60% of the surface area of Latin America and have more than 200 million citizens.

Andean Pact. It was created in 1969 by Colombia, Ecuador, Bolivia, Peru and Venezuela.

CACM: The Central American Common Market. It was created in December 1960 by the following countries: Nicaragua, El Salvador, Guatemala and Honduras. In 1962 Costa Rica and Panama joined and Honduras withdrew in 1971.

7.4. AFRICA

One of the most significant treaties of the African Economic Community is the AEC. It was established in 1991 in Nigeria, where 51 African states joined. The intention of the treaty was to become an economic unit. The idiosyncrasies of the African continent make it difficult to be optimistic about the achievement of this treaty, also due to the great corruption that exists in most of the member countries.

The 51 member countries that make up the CAA are: Algeria, Angola, Benin, Botswana, Burkina Faso, Burundi, Cameroon, Cameroon, Cape Verde, Central African Republic, Chad, Comoros, Congo, Democratic Republic of Congo, Côte d'Ivoire, Djibouti, Egypt, Equatorial Guinea, Eritrea, Ethiopia, Gabon, Gambia, Ghana, Guinea Conakry, Kenya, Lesotho, Liberia, Libya, Madagascar, Malawi, Mali, Mali, Mauritania, Mauritius, Mozambique, Namibia, Niger, Nigeria, Rwanda, Arab Democratic Republic of Sharawia, Sao Tome and Principe, Senegal, Seychelles, Sierra Leone, Somalia, South Africa, Sudan, Swaziland, Tanzania, Togo, Tunisia, Uganda, Zambia, Zimbabwe.

7.5. ASIA

Today it is the most economically dynamic continent, especially China and Japan. The most important treaty is ASEAN, created in 1967 and comprising the Philippines, Indonesia, Malaysia, Brunei, Burma, Laos, Singapore and Thailand. The crisis that erupted in the region from 1997 onwards stimulated the search for new consultation mechanisms that would boost economic and political relations in the countries of the region. It was in this context that ASEAN+3 was created, comprising the ASEAN countries plus China, South Korea and Japan, with the aim of creating a regional platform for dialogue, consultation, exchange and cooperation between the nations of Northeast and Southeast Asia.

Japan. Two decades ago, Japan's economy stagnated. Since the new millennium it has begun to grow at moderate rates and with a trade balance in surplus. It is a very competitive market, especially in technology. For a company that values quality in its products, it is a reference market to export to.

China. Today it is the engine of the world economy. Its data is relentless:

- The economy has annual growth rates of 8-10%.
- It is one of the world's leading exporting countries.
- It attracts most foreign investment.
- Its economy is on a par with that of Japan and the United States.
- It is one of the countries that buys the most foreign debt from industrialised countries, including Spain.
- Most analysts agree that China will go through a similar process to Japan, albeit on a much larger scale.
- Today, it has several global brands (China Mobile, Lenovo).

China's entry into the WTO in 2001 was the key to the great opening to world trade, in addition to the great showcase of the Shanghai Olympics in 2008 and the International Expo in 2010.

India. When we talk about China, almost everyone understands that it is the world's factory. With India it is similar, although the approach is different. India is investing much more in research and services (more than 50% of GDP comes from the service sector). So there is no doubt that India is the laboratory of the world. Its economic growth is unstoppable, albeit in slightly smaller numbers than China. Another difference between India and China is its protectionist policy regarding the entry of foreign products and investments by European and American companies. The Indian economy is specialising in information and communication technologies (ICTs) and offshoring (offshoring of services), especially call centres for financial and technological services. The Indian human resources market offers highly skilled engineers and programmers, as well as English language skills.

One of the most prestigious rankings is published annually by the World Economic Forum, through the competitive growth index, i.e. the macroeconomic environment of each country, the situation of its public institutions and the use of technology. The countries that have topped this ranking in recent years are: Nordic countries such as Sweden and Finland, and the United States. The classification by groups of countries is made taking into account the size of the economy, growth expectations, foreign investment, wage levels, labour force, foreign trade, exchange rates, among others. According to these criteria, six country groups can be established.

> The World Economic Forum is an independent international organisation committed to improving the state of the world by engaging business, political leaders, academics and others in society to shape global, regional and industry agendas.

- Highly developed countries block: Those countries that sustain a high per capita income, as well as a strong and dynamic economy at the global level. These countries account for the largest share of international trade in value-added products. These countries are called the G-7: the United States, Japan, Germany, France, the United Kingdom, Italy and Canada.
- Block of emerging countries: These are the countries whose economies are showing strong growth year after year, although they are currently growth markets and have medium- to long-term potential. These countries are called BRIC (Brazil, Russia, India and China).
- Developed countries bloc: In addition to the G7, there are a number of OECD countries, such as Australia, Spain, Belgium, Sweden, etc., which have stable and outward-looking economies, although they are not large enough economically to be considered among the seven world economies.
  - Bloc of other emerging countries: These are countries that have achieved an industrial and commercial strength that enables them to compete with other developed countries, e.g. South Korea, Poland, Turkey, Mexico, South Africa, etc.

- Developing countries or Third World bloc: These are countries that, due to their historical trajectory, have a technological level or per capita income that is much lower than that of developed countries. However, given favourable political conditions and an open economic policy, they tend to initiate a process of industrialisation. We can cite some Maghreb or Arab countries, as well as Latin American countries. To this group we could add European countries such as Romania or Bulgaria.

- Block of least developed countries or Fourth World: These are countries with a very low per capita income that has no signs of improving in the medium term. They are usually countries in a state of poverty and the country's own internal conflicts make it very difficult for them to recover. We can cite many African countries (Angola, Senegal, etc.), Central American countries such as Haiti, one of the countries most affected by natural disasters and which has increased its poverty, and Asian countries such as Cambodia.

9. POTENTIAL AREAS AND MARKETS

Technological change, the emergence of the hyper-information society and globalisation mean that companies find themselves in increasingly open and dynamic environments, where competition is intensifying and change is permanent and accelerated. At the same time, changes in environmental conditions and their increasing complexity are shaping radically different rules of fire and are creating a bewilderment in organisations in the face of this uncertainty. This is leading to the following conclusions:

- Globalisation of both supply and demand markets, favoured by almost non-existent barriers to entry, due to administrative deregulation, existing information and deteriorating respect for competition.
- Convergence between industries enabling the development of new business models, e.g. telecommunications and IT.
- The development of the hyper-consumer society, with the development of large distribution companies based on speed, continuous innovation in product assortment, excellence in the standardisation of operational processes and the achievement of low prices, the attractiveness of the continuous renovation of their establishments, and which will be reinforced by the emergence of e-commerce.
- The rapid emergence in developing countries of mega-corporations such as in Southeast Asia.
- The maturation and relocation of traditional industries in developed countries, especially local or regional companies, in the face of competition from low-cost countries, as well as the immigration of people from these countries,

➢ The continuous emergence of new, fast-growing and profitable niches, based on services (health, aesthetics, leisure), elite or premium products and services (leisure and luxury consumption) or new technology products and services. . However, these niches have increasingly shorter life cycles.

➢ Increasing mergers and acquisitions between companies to reach a more global size and accelerate the achievement of greater competitive differentiation.

➢ Promoting innovation as a driver of growth and a source of disruptive technologies.

According to the McKinsey report, the evolutionary outlook for 2050 envisages a society in profound transformation in terms of technological, social and business models. In particular, new technologies such as IT and telecommunications will promote an extraordinary transformation in social and business habits and values. As a consequence of globalisation, geographical barriers are being reduced. World trade accounts for about 25% of world GDP. Historically, capital flows used to originate in developed nations to take advantage of opportunities in emerging countries. Now, these countries are becoming net exporters of capital. While borders between countries still exist, they are increasingly irrelevant at the trade level. The global trends for the 21st century could therefore be summarised as follows:

Economic activity is shifting dramatically towards Asia. Over the next 30 years, there is a shift of wealth towards the United States and Asia, which will account for more than 50% of global GDP. The United States will remain the fastest growing economy in absolute terms over the next 20 years. Asia, today, excluding Japan, accounts for 12% of world GDP, while Western Europe accounts for 30%. In 20 years' time they will be at the same level.

670 million people in Asia will exceed an income of $5,000 per family per year over the next decade. By 2025, in China, it will be 75% of the population.

Population growth and the development of emerging nations increase pressure on natural resources. Population growth and economic growth lead to increased consumption of energy and raw materials, especially oil, and a rise in resource prices.

New opportunities and a new type of consumer. The number of active consumers in the global market will increase from 1 billion to 2 billion, and 67% of these 1 billion will come from China, India and Brazil. Consumer typology is complicated by the increase of market segments. Developed markets will become increasingly complex and polarised.

This new environment presents numerous sectoral, demographic and demographic opportunities. The United States and Asia are the two areas with the greatest growth potential. New sectors such as sustainability and environment are emerging. The segment of people over 50 years of age is growing, consumers with high purchasing power and consumption capacity. The trend will be the formation of single-person households.

The incorporation of technology has transformed the way we live and interact. It is not yet possible to imagine the changes that await us as a result of advances in nanotechnology and biotechnology, but perhaps even more important is their impact on the transformation of social habits. Fifteen years ago, mobile phones were barely known, and not even twenty years ago laptops. Already 5% of world trade uses the Internet and 70% of European consumers use the Internet for shopping. The way companies work is changing, you can be connected 7 days a week, 24 hours a day. Today, through teleworking, it is possible for many people to work thousands of kilometres away from their companies.

Knowledge is an increasingly important factor in differentiating companies. Knowledge is accelerating and innovation is becoming a cornerstone of corporate success. Information storage is growing without limit and the amount of knowledge created every second has broken all ceilings and is becoming universal.

The evolution of competition between sectors in an increasingly global market is manifested in several dimensions. The first major change is that the frontier of the individual firm is becoming less relevant. It is increasingly necessary to involve other organisations in the process of creating goods and services, and companies must seek opportunities to collaborate with industry leaders to secure a leading position in their sector. Secondly, the consumer is being incorporated into the product generation process.

A third trend is the breaking down of barriers between sectors, especially visible in the industries associated with the digital world. And along with industries that are opening up, new business models are emerging based on a very notable specialisation with companies capable of performing very specific tasks, thanks to which they become true global leaders. Finally, the role of Private Equity goes beyond that of mere capital providers. They have become agents of value creation by restructuring companies all over the world.

The global battle for talent. Until now, domestic talent pools in developed countries have been sufficient to meet demand. The shrinking working-age population in developed countries will mean that these pools will no longer be sufficient. Over the next 15 years, 3 million fewer Spaniards will enter the labour market, but there will be a greater availability of talent in developing countries. China and India currently account for 50% of young university graduates in developing countries.

Bipolarisation of the FMCG market. Fragmentation into micro-segments is taking place. In addition, there is greater consumer influence thanks to technology that allows them to know about products. There is a growth in the power of large-scale distribution with respect to manufacturers, the power of the brand and trust in it, and the importance of on-line shopping.

> Latin America presents a particularly attractive opportunity for Spanish companies due to its cultural proximity.

Keys to maintaining the success of Spain and its companies:

➢ Internationalisation: In recent years, many Spanish companies have become global multinationals and are therefore more relevant worldwide. It is increasingly common to see global operations led by Spanish companies (Telefónica, Altadis, Banco Santander).

➢ Competitiveness: Asian countries exert great pressure on Spain because of their low costs, as does India. Foreign investment in Spain has fallen by 40% and reflects a loss of competitiveness . To meet this challenge, it will be key to take advantage of the opportunities arising from improvements in the efficiency of internal processes and operations, as well as outsourcing and relocation opportunities.

➢ Innovation: Spanish investment in R&D&I is half that of France or Germany. One fifth of Spanish GDP will have to reinvent itself to protect itself from the unstoppable trend of moving labour-intensive industries to emerging countries: computers, steel, textiles, footwear, fashion, ceramics, automobiles. All these sectors are highly vulnerable, as most of these products will be manufactured in developing countries.

> In Spain, productivity per worker is 56,000 dollars per year, below countries such as Germany and the United Kingdom, which is 62,000 dollars, and far below the 91,000 dollars in the United States.

9.1. BRIC COUNTRIES

There is a new world order that has taken the world by surprise, ushering in the new internationalisation of economies and the recent process of modern democracies. This new scenario leaves the United States behind in its leadership. Europe and Asia are vying to take the reins of international trade. The 21st century seems to be experiencing a true geopolitical revolution. Globalisation is generating, on the one hand, the global distribution of political power and, on the other, the centralisation of economic power in transnational corporations. This has given rise to emerging economies. One of the most important emerging blocs at the moment is the BRIC (Brazil, Russia, India and China).

Emerging market economies play an increasingly important role in global economic development. After the crises in Asia, Russia, Brazil, Turkey and Argentina in the late 1990s, interest in the economic and financial potential in emerging market economies has become more pronounced, especially in the BRICs, as these four economies in demographic and economic terms represent the world's great economic potential.

According to several reports, in the next 50 years the BRIC economies could become a very important bloc in the world economy, even larger than the G-7. However, the population of this bloc will remain poorer on average, with the exception of China, which could reach income levels per capita like the developed economies. In view of China's differentiating growth, global interest has focused on its development. There is no doubt in any report about China's or India's growth, but Russia's growth leaves some doubt. Russia's economy is based on oil, gas and mineral extraction, and is therefore more sensitive to international market fluctuations. Brazil has had periods of high growth, although so far there are no signs of it being permanent.

> The contribution of these countries, in terms of GDP in the world economy, remains relatively small (8%). The G7 accounts for 65%.

The BRICs' global economic weight increases significantly due to their much lower price levels. From this perspective, the share of these countries is 24%. Another characteristic of their economic development is that their growth has fluctuated more than in developed countries. Such fluctuations have marked the cycles of the world economy. Standards of living and prosperity in these countries have risen considerably. In particular, China has increased its GDP per capita twelvefold, India has quadrupled, Brazil has doubled and Russia has had a smaller impact.

□ **Growth factors**: The form of economic development of countries such as Japan or Germany has not had much to do with the characteristics of these countries. The main characteristics of China's high economic growth have been the strong inflow of foreign capital into its economy, mostly expressed in the form of foreign direct investment, as well as the increase in labour productivity and technological progress of its productive apparatus. A similar pattern of growth can be found in India, where employment has played an even more important role than in China. In contrast, Brazil and Russia have seen negative productivity growth in their industries. In this context it is difficult to assess Russia's growth, given the continuing imbalances in its economy. Brazil's growth is mainly based on the accelerated accumulation of factors of production. All these components contributed to growth in the United States, while employment growth has been relatively insignificant in Germany and Japan. Moreover, due to the international division of labour, increased trade also helps to sustain the growth process in less developed countries that possess an abundance of cheap labour.

Greater openness also generally increases foreign competition, and puts pressure for further reforms in other areas.

The BRIC countries have achieved a high degree of prosperity among countries that have opened their economies to the outside world. With the exception of Russia, which is susceptible to special circumstances, the rest of the BRIC countries have followed a similar pattern, where they have seen significant increases in their living standards, thanks to the greater openness of their economies, if these are measured by exports as a proportion of GDP. Especially China has experienced significant development in terms of both openness and prosperity.

□ **Population and educational growth factors**. The BRIC countries account for around 42% of the world's population. According to demographic forecasts, by 2050 the population of these countries will reach 3.4 billion citizens. The population growth will be highest in India with more than 1.5 billion inhabitants. Diseases such as AIDS will have a major impact especially in Russia, although Brazil, China and India have very high proportions compared to the West. In terms of education, Russia has a clear advantage over the rest of the world. Illiteracy is almost non-existent. Brazil and China are at around 10-15 per cent. However, in the latter two countries, the younger generations have a much higher level of education than previous generations. India, on the other hand, has the highest level of adult illiteracy, although its workforce is tending towards skilled work (relocation of Western companies in the technology and science sector).

The map of the world economy is therefore being restructured. In 2050, the most powerful economies will no longer be the same, so companies' geopolitical and economic strategies will have to adapt to this new scenario.

> The key element of these patterns is that better growth is achieved by economic liberalisation, allowing the free movement of factors of production goods, and facilitating greater access to capital and technology.

☐ **China and India**. The resurgence of these countries can be seen as a true economic revolution. From being of no significance in the world economy, they have become leading economic players. The fundamental differences between China and India and the rest of the more industrialised countries are mainly related to the economic approach: China and India have been primarily agrarian economies, making it very difficult for them to compete with an industrial economy. China was able to adapt from a communist system to a more open economy than few people suspected. This policy of openness, together with globalisation, has led to economic growth. Due to their potential, especially in terms of labour force, these countries will be able to determine the future of the world economy; moreover, they are determining the world economic cycles in the short and medium term. China's economic growth has been based on promoting exports, with the potential of a large labour force that reduces the economic cost of manufacturing to a very low level. This has led to a growth in the standard of living of the average citizen and massive movements from towns to cities. India's growth has come about through the rationalisation of its domestic economy, as well as the export of ICT (Information and Communication Technology) products.

> Today, China contributes more than 55 million labour masses to the world, while India provides more than 85 million workers. The United States and Europe together account for about 15 million workers.

We can affirm that one of the most successful initiatives in China has been the modernisation of infrastructures, the first basic step for a developing country to be able to attract foreign investment and domestic development.

All the competition in China's large domestic market has only made costs lower and manufacturing cheaper. Over time, the average citizen's standard of living will rise to higher wage levels and they will organise themselves into trade unions that have a voice in government.

In India, economic liberalisation has been built around an established private sector and commercial class, with even local entrepreneurs establishing multinationals. Migratory movements from both China and India have favoured the international expansion of these countries. However, both countries are encouraging their citizens to return to their home countries to boost the domestic economy. Both India and China have a challenge ahead, which is to boost their savings rate in order to modernise their domestic infrastructures to increase their growth rate. Both countries still have a further phase of exporting services, which will bring a new scenario in the global economy.

> The BRIC countries have strengthened themselves in a strategic grouping vis-à-vis the United States and Europe.

According to the most relevant analyses, China and India are really the countries to watch, as they are transforming the global strategic order. On the other hand, these large economies are not self-sufficient in natural resources, especially China, so resource scarcity will increase costs. Globalisation could be slowed down by exogenous or endogenous forces in the United States and Europe. A slowdown in the international economy could slow down the development of these countries, although their economic progress can no longer be reversed. Maintaining sustained growth rates over time is the big question mark that is not clearly in sight in these countries. They will need to establish changes in the financial sector and maintain sustained savings, as well as reduce dependence on single-product economies, such as Russia's dependence on oil. The constant challenges for these economies and the rest of the countries in a globalised market remain the same: more openness, better infrastructure and education.

CONCLUSIONS

The internationalisation of the company is the first step towards competing in the global market. In terms of the competencies that a company must have in order to compete, we can cite the professionalisation of human resources, coherent company image and corporate economies of scale. The company must identify the new global political and economic framework, with the importance of the BRIC countries that define the world economic cycles in addition to the United States and Europe. Today the company must understand the global economy, social scenarios, and cultural and political influences.

There is no doubt that the international trade context directly and indirectly influences the company. For all these reasons, it is essential for the internationalisation of the company to situate itself in this global context. All national and international institutions promote knowledge of international trade, offering guidelines and regulations so that all the economic agents involved respect the uses and rules recognised by most countries.

The international economy is currently going through a key period for the new organigram of geopolitics and the global economy. The BRIC countries stand out in this influence, especially China and India, which are showing clear signs that they will be the leaders of this new bloc of countries competing with the United States and Europe.

ABOUT THE AUTHOR

José-Nicanor Pinilla Barcelona comes from a village in Zaragoza, Spain, Brea de Aragón, where shoes have been manufactured for generations. This has influenced his business outlook and entrepreneurial spirit. He has a business career of more than 30 years, and as a teacher and consultant in international trade since learning by teaching is his main vocation. For more information visit his LinkedIN profile: https://www.linkedin.com/in/escueladelemprendedor/